EASY HOME WINEMAKING

by

John David Hutto

ALL AMERICAN PRESS

How to make excellent wine for about $1.50 per gallon is explained from start to finish. Readily available and inexpensive ingredients are suggested, as are budget sources for utensils and storage containers. A basic recipe for a medium-bodied medium-dry wine is furnished, plus some suggestions for modification to taste.

This method recommends the use of commercial fruit juice and does **not** require the hassle associated with using fresh fruit. How to make wine using fresh fruit **is** explained, however, in case you prefer that approach.

"A loaf of bread,
a jug of wine,
and thou"

Omar Khayýam

Cataloging In Publication Data

Library of Congress Catalog Card Number:
87-71565

International Standard Book Number:
0-940879-02-6

TABLE OF CONTENTS

PREFACE

Home winemaking has become big business! Many cities have specialty shops selling winemaking supplies, and mail order houses have been selling winemaking equipment for years.

There are two problems with a novice winemaker patronizing these establishments: (1) You can easily become overwhelmed by the amount of equipment available (and that you will probably be told that you need) and (2) You can easily become discouraged by the amount of expense involved.

Save trips to the winemaking specialty shops until later. First, make wine my way — the simple/cheap way. Your investment in equipment will be minimal; the ingredients I recommend are plentiful and economical; and the resulting wine will be delicious (for sure) and potent (if you want it to be)!

My method includes options so that you can make your own style of wine with only a few simple adjustments to the basic method.

Follow these instructions carefully and in just a few short weeks you will be enjoying your own delicious wine for approximately $1.50 per gallon (1987 dollars).

GENERAL INFORMATION ABOUT WINE

BRIEF HISTORY

In early times wine had a much more practical reason for existence than just the pure pleasure of drinking. Early civilizations discovered that those who drank fermented juice did not get sick as often as those who drank the impure water. This reason for wine drinking continues today in many under-developed countries.

Wine is mentioned often in the Bible and has come down through the ages as a part of many religions. Catholic, Jewish and Protestant ceremonies all include wine as some part of their rituals.

HOW WINE IS MADE

Wine is the fermented juice of the grape or other fruit. Commercially, the fruit is crushed, with care taken to avoid crushing the seeds. The juice, referred to as must, is allowed to ferment in wooden vats for a period of time, dependent upon the amount of sugar contained in the fruit and the type of wine being produced. The longer fermentation is allowed to continue, the drier the wine.

VINTAGE YEARS

Be aware that vintage years mean very little to all but the most knowledgeable wine connoisseurs. What was a "very good year" for one vineyard may have been a disaster for the vineyard next door, for a variety of reasons. The only way to tell whether a wine is good or not is to smell it and taste it. There are details about this in the **HOW TO TASTE WINE** chapter.

AGING

White wine does not improve with aging after about three years. Even red wine will reach an optimum age around nine or ten years, and, if left in the barrel or bottle beyond that time, will go bad. Buyers never open those ancient bottles of wine that are auctioned off from time to time, but if they did, they would probably find vinegar! In general, once a bottle of wine has been opened, it should be consumed within a short period of time. It is possible to reseal a partially full bottle of wine, however. The details are provided in the **BOTTLING** chapter.

COOKING WITH WINE

Since alcohol will evaporate when heated, it serves no useful purpose to add wine to food while it is cooking. If a recipe calls for wine to be added, add it **after** the cooking is done.

STAYING LEGAL

Current Federal law (1987) allows each adult to produce up to 100 gallons of wine per year for personal use. There is also a household limit of 200 gallons per year. There are no record keeping requirements as long as you stay within these limits.

State laws do not necessarily parallel Federal laws as they pertain to this activity. In fact, they vary widely. Although the winemaking described in this book is strictly for hobby purposes, it would be advisable to check with your state and local authorities as to any regulations that may exist.

Such state authorities will likely be located in the revenue or tax department. The appropriate Federal authorities are located in the Alcohol, Tobacco and Firearms Bureau of the United States Treasury Department.

CAUTION

The winemaking process consists of yeast attacking sugar and converting the sugar into alcohol. This chemical reaction is called fermentation and creates carbon dioxide gas (CO_2). This gas pressure must be allowed to escape. It is absolutely essential that all chemical action be complete before any wine is bottled. Failure to do this can cause bursting of the bottle containing the wine, at some unpredictable time, and could result in bodily injury to anyone nearby.

The method described in this book, if followed to the letter, is completely safe. I have personally made both wine and beer, using this method, with absolutely no problems. The airlock, to be described later in this book, allows all gas to escape harmlessly. It also prevents the entry of wild yeasts, which are potentially harmful to the wine. Another very important function of the airlock is a visual indication as to when all chemical action has stopped.

Use of the airlock, along with the prudent exercise of patience, will guarantee that your winemaking venture will be both fun and safe.

UTENSILS REQUIRED

Certain utensils are required during the actual winemaking steps and for storage later. In keeping with the statements made in the **PREFACE,** the suggestions made here are for items both economical and readily available.

WINEMAKING UTENSILS

For dissolving sugar, a large metal cookpot and a long-handled spoon are needed. These are probably in your kitchen already. A medium-sized funnel is needed to pour sugar-water and other ingredients into a five-gallon glass bottle. A suitable glass bottle is the type used on old-timey water coolers in older office buildings. Likely sources for these bottles are older hardware stores and lawn and garden shops. While there is some cost involved here it should only be a few dollars and represents an investment that can be used indefinitely.

Other items needed include a cork to fit the neck of the glass bottle; a three-foot piece of plastic tubing to insert through the cork for pressure release; a coffee cup for preparing a yeast culture; a soft drink bottle about three-fourths full of water to use as a one-way medium for gas pressure release; a candle for sealing the cork and tube; and a match for lighting the candle.

This strange combination of items will be explained completely in the **BASIC RECIPE** chapter. Some substitutions can be made for the above, especially pertaining to the five-gallon glass bottle. For example, a plastic jug or bottle could be used. I don't recommend it though, because the plastic will affect the taste of the wine to some extent. Also, you could use a vessel of lesser capacity than five gallons. I don't recommend this either. Since there is some trouble involved in winemaking, why not make enough wine at one time for it to be worthwhile?

The point is that, while I am telling you a way to make wine simply and cheaply, I am leaving you the flexibility to improvise, yet still be successful.

STORAGE CONTAINERS

For storage you can use empty store-bought wine bottles. If you don't happen to have 20 empty wine bottles lying around, then go see your neighborhood druggist. He will probably have some empty one-gallon medicine bottles which he will be glad to give you. These are especially nice because they are usually dark brown and, therefore, protect the wine during long storage periods. They are also free! Do be careful to wash medicine bottles thoroughly before using them, however.

Following is a summary of all utensils needed:

SUMMARY OF UTENSILS NEEDED

1 Large Cookpot

1 Long-Handled Spoon

1 Medium-Sized Funnel

1 5-Gallon Glass Bottle

1 Cork

1 3-Foot Plastic Tubing

1 Coffee Cup

1 Soft Drink Bottle

1 Candle

Lot Matches

Lot Storage Bottles

INGREDIENTS REQUIRED

As mentioned earlier, this book explains a simple failure-proof way to make wine very cheaply. However, there are infinite ways to introduce variations. The basic ingredients I am about to list, and the basic recipe to be explained in the next chapter, will work without fail every time. It is suggested that you purchase these exact ingredients and combine them precisely as explained, at least **the first time.** Once you have proven to yourself how easy it is to produce wine, then you can start customizing the process. There will even be some suggested changes in the **VARIATIONS** chapter.

At the end of this chapter is a list of the ingredients required to make five gallons of a medium-bodied red wine. Depending upon how the sugar is introduced, this wine can be dry, medium-dry or sweet.

These ingredients should cost about $8.00 (1987 dollars). Dividing $8.00 by five gallons yields a per-gallon cost of around $1.50, less sales tax. This is already much cheaper than store-bought wine, but it gets even better. For example, you'll never have to buy yeast again, for two reasons. First, the package of yeast has several individual packets inside. You only need a pinch of yeast out of one of the packets to get the fermentation process started. Therefore, the initial yeast purchase will last a long time. If you should choose to keep a batch of wine working at all times, you can start batch number two, without any yeast, by dipping out a little of batch number one and adding it to batch number two, etc.

Also, there are other mediums you can use in place of store-bought grape juice. Many of these are left over from your normal cooking activities and are therefore "free" to the winemaking process. There will be more on this aspect in the **VARIATIONS** chapter.

INGREDIENTS REQUIRED

3 40-Ounce Bottles Red Grape Juice
Or
2 64-Ounce Bottles Red Grape Juice

10 Pounds Sugar

1 Package Baker's Yeast

5 Gallons Of Water

BASIC RECIPE

STEP ONE

Refer to the **UTENSILS** and **INGREDIENTS** chapters and assemble all required items in your kitchen. Place about one gallon of water over high heat using the metal cookpot. When the water is boiling vigorously, stir in about one-third of the sugar (three to three and one half pounds), stirring it with the long-handled spoon until it is completely dissolved.

Using the funnel, pour all of the grape juice into the glass bottle followed by the sugar-water solution. Do not pour the sugar-water solution in until it has cooled because it might break the bottle.

Next, prepare a yeast culture as follows: Run some warm (not hot) tap water into the coffee cup. If the water is too hot it will harm or kill the yeast. Stir in a small amount of yeast from one of the yeast packets. The absolute amount is optional, but the more yeast used, the more of a yeasty taste the finished wine will have. For my taste, the least amount of yeast necessary to start the fermentation process, the better. After the yeast culture is prepared, pour it into the bottle with the grape juice and sugar solution.

Shake all the ingredients and you will have completed step one of the basic recipe. So far you should have the glass bottle approximately half full of: All the grape juice, one-third of the sugar, the yeast culture, and water. Add enough water to bring the level of the bottle up to about three gallons, but **no more.** The rest of the sugar will be added in two additional stages. Each stage will require about one gallon of water to dissolve the sugar. Therefore, there must be sufficient room left in the bottle to absorb this additional liquid.

It would be a good idea at this time to move the bottle to the place where it will remain during the fermentation process. With three gallons of liquid inside, the bottle should weigh approximately 30 pounds. For the comfort of the wine you should choose a location that is dark and pleasantly warm. For your own comfort you should choose a place that is somewhat removed from living and sleeping quarters. This is because there will be some odor and some sound as fermentation takes place. The odor is actually not unpleasant — it is similar to overripe fruit with a hint of yeast thrown in. The sound is a rather pleasant bubbling noise, but it might disturb you if you were trying to sleep. In choosing your location, bear in mind that complete fermentation can take several months. An out-of-the-way place in a heated basement would be ideal.

STEP TWO

The next step requires setting up the airlock. Refer to ILLUSTRATION I while reading these instructions.

ILLUSTRATION I

With the glass bottle in its final resting place, insert the plastic tube through the cork. Use an ice-pick, or equivalent, to create an opening through the cork. Next, using candle wax, seal the tube to the cork so that there will be no air leakage. This seal is very important. Without it, there will be no indication as to whether fermentation is occurring, or whether it has stopped.

Next, insert the cork, with tube attached, into the neck of the glass bottle. Fill the soft drink bottle about three-fourths full of water, set it next to the large bottle, and insert the free end of the plastic tube into the soft drink bottle below the level of the water. This is the airlock.

As fermentation takes place, the gas that is formed passes through the plastic tube, bubbles up through the water in the soft drink bottle, and escapes harmlessly into the air. The water in the soft drink bottle acts as a one-way valve. Even though the gas created inside the winemaking bottle can get out, nothing can get inside. This prevents any wild yeasts from turning the wine into vinegar. Be sure that the water in the soft drink bottle does not evaporate because the airlock will not work without it.

As mentioned earlier, another important function of the airlock is to give a visual indication that fermentation is occurring, and when it has stopped. During the early stages of fermentation, the bubbling of the gas escaping will be vigorous. Toward the end of the process, the bubbling will subside. As warned in the **CAUTION** chapter, you must not bottle any wine until all fermentation (bubbling) has stopped. Even then you will want to wait for quite some time before bottling, so that the sediment will have time to collect on the bottom of the bottle. Even the basic recipe, which uses store-bought grape juice, will take several days (maybe even weeks) before the wine is clear and has any polish to it.

STEPS THREE AND FOUR

At this point, however, the actual recipe has not yet been completed. There is still the remaining sugar to be introduced into the process. After the initial bubbling, resulting from the start-up procedure, subsides (but before it has stopped completely) you should add the second one-third of sugar. This should come after about one week to ten days. As before, dissolve the sugar in about one gallon of water. After it cools, add it to the five-gallon bottle. There should now be about four gallons of liquid in the bottle.

Again, wait several days until the bubbling has almost stopped, and add the last of the sugar. Of course, as before, dissolve it in a gallon of water and let it cool before pouring it in. Adding the sugar in stages like this allows the yeast to convert the maximum amount of sugar into alcohol. An alcohol content of eight to ten percent is probable using baker's yeast. A stronger alcoholic content is possible, if desired, using winemaking yeast.

If you prefer a sweet wine with less alcohol, you can add all the sugar at once. The yeast will not be able to handle all the sugar under this condition, and fermentation will stop while unconverted sugar is still present. This results in a much sweeter wine and will finish working faster, in case you are in a hurry.

Still another method is to add the sugar in two stages instead of three. This will result in a medium-sweet (or medium-dry) wine, somewhere between the two extremes. Having tried it all three ways, I prefer the driest variety.

FINAL STEP

The final step in the winemaking process is the hardest, especially the first time. It is, of course, the waiting. The actual time it will take from start to finish will vary due to differences in temperature, atmospheric pressure, location, etc. It could take three months or more. Again, do **not** bottle any wine until there is absolutely **no** bubble activity through the airlock. During the final stages, a given gas bubble can take a long time to form and give an indication through the airlock. Therefore, watch closely and be careful.

After all fermentation has stopped you could immediately transfer the wine into smaller containers for storage. However, if you do, sediment will collect in the bottom of each storage bottle as the wine settles. A better way is to leave the wine undisturbed in the original five-gallon bottle. Let it settle until the wine is clear and all residue is on the bottom. The **BOTTLING** chapter will explain how to transfer the wine into individual bottles without disturbing the sediment.

By the way, even though the wine will still be somewhat cloudy at this point, it is perfectly all right to drink. You may want to draw off a glass, or even a bottle, to test your level of success. It won't be quite as good as when it is clear, but it will do!

BOTTLING

Bottling can be done in either one or two basic steps. You can wait until the sediment has collected in the bottom of the large winemaking vessel, and bottle direct into individual wine bottles. Or, you can bottle from the winemaking vessel into larger storage containers, e.g., the medicine bottles suggested in the **UTENSILS REQUIRED** chapter. Using this method, you can either wait for all settling to stop, or bottle at some intermediate time. Bottling before settling is complete will require more care when the transfer to individual wine bottles is done. If possible, I recommend that you wait until settling is complete. I have tried it both ways and it works better that way.

Settling is easy to monitor. As the sediment slowly sinks to the bottom of the bottle, a distinct horizontal line will be apparent. Above this line the wine will be clear and will have a certain amount of polish, discernible even through glass. Below the line the wine will still be cloudy. Should you desire a bottle of wine to drink during this period, you can easily draw off a bottle from the clear section. Details about how to do this are furnished in the **STORAGE** chapter.

In bottling wine, the major objective is to transfer it to other containers without stirring up the sediment. There is only one way to do this and that is by using a siphon. You **could** use the same plastic tube you used as part of the airlock, but please don't. It would take forever and it would not be fair to others who might drink your wine. Instead, buy a siphon. Most drugstores sell a mechanical siphon that consists of an input tube, an output tube, and a squeeze bulb. If you can't find one of these in a drugstore or variety store, the nearest winemaking supply store will surely have one. It is an inexpensive item that will make bottling your wine much easier.

If you decide to use medicine bottles for storage, they come with screw on caps. If you decide to bottle some wine in individual wine bottles, you might have some that require corking. It could be difficult to get a good seal between the cork and bottle without the use of a special corkpuller. See ILLUSTRATION II, on page 20, for a sketch of this special item.

This corkpuller is not a corkscrew. A corkscrew puts a hole through the cork. This tool does not. To put a cork in a bottle, you place the cork between the legs of the corkpuller and insert the longer leg into the bottle. Next, you insert the other leg so that both legs are inside the neck of the bottle with the cork squeezed between them.

With a gentle twisting motion, the cork can be gently pushed all the way into the neck of the bottle. By slightly rocking the corkpuller back-and-forth while pulling, the corkpuller can be removed without disturbing the cork. To remove a cork, simply reverse the procedure. This handy little gadget can also be used to reseal a wine bottle once it has been opened.

ILLUSTRATION II

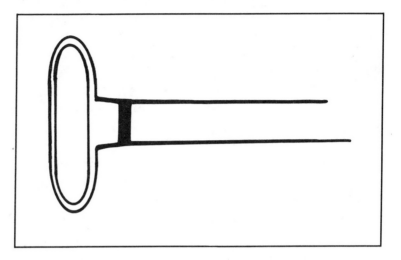

Any winemaking store should have this item in stock. If you have trouble finding it, you can order one from any winery in California. That's where I got mine. It cost $3.95 (1987 dollars).

STORAGE

Once the wine is bottled, whether in large containers, individual bottles, or in some combination of the two, it should be kept in a cool, dark, but readily accessible place. If settling is not complete at the time of bottling, be aware that movement, such as that required to draw off a bottle to serve, may stir up some sediment. Be sure to select your storage place with this in mind.

I have found that a pantry or closet inside the living quarters of the house is an ideal storage location for soon-to-be-drunk wine. A basement is excellent for long-term storage.

Contrary to popular opinion, I have found that the position of the bottles during storage makes no difference as far as wine quality is concerned. Storing bottles on their sides does serve to keep the corks moist, however, thereby making for a tighter seal.

VARIATIONS

The utensils, ingredients, and basic recipe recommended in this book are for a fail-safe wine. They were recommended and described in a certain manner so that the first-time winemaker would be successful. A success the first time out builds confidence and prepares the individual for more adventurous methods, some of which are described below.

VARIATIONS ON BASIC RECIPE

Among the endless variations possible, using the basic recipe, is the substitution of other mediums for the red bottled grape juice. Among the most obvious substitutions is frozen concentrate in place of the bottled variety. Or, staying with grape, you could make white wine instead of red wine by using bottled white grape juice, which is readily available. You can add more or less juice and/or sugar to vary the body and/or dryness.

Numerous other commercial juices are available, most of which will make good wine. Among the possibilities are apple, peach, cherry, various kinds of berry juices, etc. In fact, about the only juice that won't make wine is juice that has had some type of preservative added to retard spoilage. Since attack by yeast is considered "spoilage" in the commercial fruit juice industry, the preservative will kill the yeast you deliberately add to start the fermentation process. All you have to do to avoid this problem is to use only juices that have no preservatives. The presence of preservatives should be clearly stated on the label.

OTHER VARIATIONS

Most people don't realize it but vegetables will make wine too. In fact almost any edible organic matter will ferment and make wine. Think about it. Most whiskies are made from grain. Rye is made from rye, bourbon from corn, vodka from wheat (sometimes potatoes), sake from rice, etc. The only real difference from wine is that whiskey goes through an additional step, that of distillation. Otherwise, the mash that results before the distillation step is the same as wine must. If allowed to settle and age somewhat, many of these mashes are very good to drink.

Even certain flowers will make wine, e.g., dandelion wine and rose petal wine. After you have mastered the basic technique, let your imagination take over and be inventive!

There are several reasons why I recommend store-bought ingredients for your first winemaking venture. To be successful is the most obvious reason, but it goes deeper than that. Using commercial ingredients assures success because you start with a sterile product. The addition of the yeast is under

23

your control. Also, using commercial products is convenient. Imagine having to go out and pick fruit before you could start! Nevertheless, if you are a hard-working, adventurous type, there are many other methods of making wine.

ORIGINAL METHOD

On a recent visit to Europe, I was paying particular attention to the wine being served. I had heard so much about the French wines that I was disappointed in them. Of course we were drinking table wines, not the famous French vintage wines.

The wines that impressed me the most were the Italian ones. In one locally-owned establishment, just north of Rome, I noticed that the wine, although it was quite good, was very cloudy. Upon asking the proprietor about it, he apparently sensed my interest in wine and took me to his "winery." In his barn, among the bales of hay, were several crocks covered with cheese cloth. He proudly pointed to one of the crocks and exclaimed "thees is-a the vino that you are-a drinking!" I nearly dropped my glass, but I did manage to maintain my composure.

The Italian man was making wine using a centuries-old method. You simply put grapes into a container, mash them up, add water, cover the container to keep the flies out, and let the wild yeasts, that are already on the grapes, take over. This method is not very sanitary but it does work.

The winemaking risk involved is that the result may be vinegar instead of wine.

SUMMARY OF VARIATIONS

Between the two extremes of my basic recipe and the Italian man's method, is an infinite number of variations you can try. After using my method first, you will have proven to yourself that it does work and it is relatively easy.

There is a lot of satisfaction to drinking your own wine at dinner. You can also have some fun with your friends and relatives if you like that sort of thing. There'll be more about that in the **FUN WITH HOMEMADE WINE** chapter.

TYPES OF WINE

Most wines are named for the places in which they were first produced. The major wine centers of Europe are Spain, France, Italy and the Rhine Valley of Germany, however, California is the largest wine-producing region in the world. Wine is also produced in several other areas of the United States, e.g., New York, Michigan and Ohio.

There are several terms used to describe wine. In many cases wines are described as being either one or the other of two contradictory terms, as described below:

RED OR WHITE

On the surface this appears obvious. However, unless the grape itself is white, it is often possible to produce white or red wine from the same grape. This is accomplished by leaving the skins in the must to produce the red variety, or leaving the skins out to produce white. The white variety will have some color, but will be much lighter in color than the red.

STILL OR SPARKLING

Still wine contains no carbon dioxide gas. All fermentation is allowed to stop before still wine is bottled. Sparkling wine does contain carbon dioxide gas. It is bottled, under controlled conditions, before all fermentation is complete. (This is not recommended for the home winemaker. See the **CAUTION** chapter.)

LIGHT OR HEAVY

Light wine contains from eight to fourteen percent alcohol. Heavy wine contains more than fourteen percent alcohol.

DRY OR SWEET

Dry wine has had all, or almost all, of the sugar converted to alcohol during fermentation. Sweet wine still contains sugar or has had sugar added.

FORTIFIED OR UNFORTIFIED

Fortified wine has had distilled spirits added to increase the alcohol content. Unfortified wine has no added spirits.

AROMATIZED OR UNAROMATIZED

Aromatized wine has had aromatic herbs and/or spices added. Unaromatized wine has had no herbs or spices added.

Following is an alphabetical list of wines, defined in the terms described above. Also furnished, if known, is the country of origin. Unless otherwise mentioned, these wines are still, unfortified and unaromatized.

ALPHABETICAL LIST OF WINES

AMONTILLADO—a type of pale dry Sherry originating in Montilla, Spain

ANGELICA—a sweet white dessert wine originating in California

BERBERA—a dry red wine

BORDEAUX—any of several red or white wines originating in the region around Bordeaux, France

BURGUNDY—any of several red or white, still or sparkling wines originating in, or around, Burgundy, France

CABERNET—a dry red wine, of French descent, made from the Cabernet Sauvignon grape

CATAWBA—a red sparkling American wine made from the Catawba grape

CHABLIS—a very dry white Burgundy wine originating in Chablis, France

CHAMPAGNE—a sparkling white wine originating in Champagne, France

CHIANTI—a dry table wine, usually red, originating in the Chianti Mountains of Italy

CLARET—a dry red table wine from the Bordeaux region of France

DUBONNET—a fortified aromatized sweet wine that originated in France

HOCK—a white Rhine wine originating in Hochheim, West Germany

LIEBFRAUMILCH—a dry white Rhine wine originating in the Rhine River valley of Germany

MADEIRA—a fortified dessert wine originating on the island of Madeira

MALAGA—a sweet white dessert wine which originated in Malaga, Spain

MANZANILLA—a pale dry Spanish Sherry, made from the Manzana apple

MARSALA—a fortified wine originating in Sicily

MOSELLE—a light dry white, still or sparkling wine, originating in the Moselle River valley of France

MUSCATEL—a sweet white wine made from Muscat grapes

PORT—a rich sweet fortified red wine originating in Oporto, Portugal

RHINE—a dry white wine originally from the Rhine River valley of Germany

ROSE'—a pink light wine made from grapes, the skins of which are removed during fermentation

SAUTERNE—a delicate sweet white wine originally from Sauterne, France

SHERRY—an amber-colored fortified wine, ranging from very dry to sweet, originally from Jerez, Spain

TOKAY—a fortified wine, made from the Tokay grape, and originating in Tokay, Hungary

VERMOUTH—a fortified aromatized sweet or dry wine, originating in France

ZINFANDEL—a white or red table wine originating in California

HOW TO TASTE WINE

There is infinitely more to tasting wine than merely drinking it. Each wine has its own unique bouquet, color, clarity, crispness, etc., all of which could be referred to as character. In order to really "taste" a wine, all of these characteristics should be deliberately experienced.

To get a real understanding of wine tasting you should visit an actual winery, either in the United States or Europe. If this is not immediately possible, this discussion should get you started.

First of all, you've probably seen people in fine restaurants smell the cork pulled from a wine bottle before accepting the wine. This worldly technique lets you know if the cork is acceptable, but tells you nothing about the wine itself. To judge the wine you must smell it and taste it.

Use a medium-sized wine glass but pour it only about half full. Make sure the glass is clean. It should not contain any soap residue and should not have been used to serve another wine since it was washed. Swirl the wine around in the glass so that it can become aerated. Now, gently smell the wine. It should have a distinct odor which is called its bouquet. The bouquet should reveal neither a hint of yeast nor any over-ripe smell.

If the wine has passed the test so far, it is now time to actually taste it. But it must be done a certain way. First, take a small amount into your mouth and swallow it quickly. At this point you are not actually attempting to taste the wine. You are conditioning your taste buds for the actual taste test which comes next.

For the actual taste test, follow this procedure: Suck, don't drink, a fair amount of wine into your mouth. The sucking action brings in oxygen along with the wine, and fully aerates the wine. Then, and only then, are you able to savor the full potential of the wine.

Under the conditions described above, if the wine is enjoyable, it can then be pronounced as acceptable.

HOW TO SERVE WINE

The classic way to serve wine is to serve red wine with red meat and white wine with white meat. In the strictest formality, at a multi-course dinner, a number of wines should be served as follows: Dry Sherry with the soup, dry white with seafood, dry red with the meat course, dry white with creamed dishes, and dry red with game. Port is good with cheese, and a sparkling or sweet wine is perfect for dessert.

Glasses should range in size from small, for the Port, to wide-brimmed, V-shaped, for the sparkling wine. Sparkling wines should always be chilled; white wines are sometimes chilled. Others should be served at room temperature.

With a mobile population, such as we have in the United States, these classic rules are changing. This is because a mobile population comes in contact with different customs, and becomes increasingly aware of numerous ways of doing things.

A safe, general rule is to serve wine that matches the texture of the meal. For example you would not want to serve a robust Burgundy (heavy, dry, and red) with a delicate entree such as crepes. Some people may like this combination, however, so a good host or hostess should ask.

Ordinarily, a sweet wine should not be served with any main course. However, the crepes example, above, would go nicely with a medium sweet wine such as a Rhine wine.

Only a few staunch wine drinkers would drink wine with dessert, but, here again, there are exceptions. In my opinion, the only hard-and-fast rule is, "if it tastes good drink it"!

Another excellent way to avoid any serious mistakes is to match the ethnic backgrounds of the entree and the wine. For example, no one could fault you for serving Chianti with spaghetti or lasagna.

One thing to remember when serving wine, is to avoid spillage. Wine will stain clothes and tablecloths but it is very easy to avoid this problem. Before taking the bottle away from the glass, give the bottle a gentle turn. This simple maneuver will roll that last drop around the mouth of the bottle and keep it from dripping on anything or anybody.

If you should spill some wine in spite of precautions, it may be possible to remove the stain before it does any permanent damage. If you will submerge the stained area in boiling water prior to normal washing, the stain will probably come out. This treatment should be restricted to white or colorfast articles due to the possibility of fading.

The real lesson to be learned in this chapter is to please yourself and your guests. Be daring. I sometimes feel that we miss a lot trying to be traditional, yes, even sophisticated. Try something unorthodox. You may create a totally unique experience.

FUN WITH HOMEMADE WINE

In addition to the fun inherent in making something for your own consumption, there are many other ways to have fun with homemade wine. Following are two stories that you may find amusing and for which you may find some application.

CHARLIE'S STORY

A friend of mine named Charlie had a lake house and was a very popular person during the summer. Not only did people drop in unexpectedly by car, but they would also come calling by boat. Of course, Charlie was expected to offer all these uninvited guests something to drink. Not only was this expensive, but he never knew how much to have on hand. The solution was homemade wine.

The basic five-gallon recipe, described in this book, was Charlie's first attempt to solve his entertainment problem. However, it soon became apparent that five gallons was a drop in the bucket when it came to serving uninvited guests. (It is not known how much of an increase in the visitation was caused by the very act of serving wine.) In any event, Charlie began searching for a method to increase his production without going over the 200 gallon annual household limitation discussed in the **STAYING LEGAL** chapter.

I don't know where he got them, but Charlie came up with two 25-gallon glass bottles! He found an out-of-the-way place in his lake house for permanent placement of these bottles. The prerequisites were that such a place had to be reachable by water hose, and had to have sufficient floor support to carry the weight.

Thereafter, Charlie kept 50 gallons of wine working or settling at all times during the summer months. This unique solution took care of serving an unknown number of unexpected guests for a very reasonable investment in time, effort and money.

MY STORY

The other story concerns something I, personally, have had fun with on several occasions. I will only relate one such incident, but there have been several, all enjoyable.

On the trip to Europe I mentioned earlier, I took several rolls of slide film. I also bought several bottles of wine to bring home, although only one made it.

After the film was developed, my wife and I invited some friends over to see our slides. Being good hosts, we always offer our guests something to drink, and this occasion was no different. We did insist, however, that their drinks be some of the

German wine that we had brought home. They agreed, and even volunteered that they considered themselves to be connoisseurs, and would critique our selection. This development made what I had in mind even better.

By now, you have probably gathered that I enjoy drinking wine. Consequently, by the time my slides came back from the developer, the German wine had long since been drunk. But I had kept the bottle, which was obviously German because of the writing on the label. Since our friends had professed to be wine connoisseurs, I decided to see how good they really were.

I had some homemade wine from white grape juice that was very similar in taste to Rhine wine. I carefully poured some of my homemade wine into the German wine bottle and recorked it with the corkpuller described in the **BOTTLING** chapter. I couldn't do anything about putting the paper back around the neck of the bottle, but I did walk back into the living room with the unopened bottle and a corkscrew in hand. I was in the process of opening what looked like a brand new bottle of wine. When I poured the wine, for all intents and purposes, I was serving authentic Rhine wine, direct from the Lorelei Rock!

Of course our friends were honored that we would share our only souvenir bottle of wine with them. What really made this funny was the way they went on about the bouquet, clarity, crispness etc.

It was all my wife and I could do to keep from laughing out loud.

You can probably find many similar ways of having fun with homemade wine. This particular joke will work best if you have kept quiet about your winemaking hobby.

SUMMARY

Home winemaking is certainly easy! It is also fun, inexpensive, and even productive. There is much satisfaction and enjoyment derived from serving guests something that you have made. This hobby also serves as an interesting conversation piece during gatherings of family and friends.

Try the basic recipe and technique described in this book. This method guarantees that you will be successful at your first attempt, and will build your confidence. Then you can go to winemaking specialty shops and spend money on sophisticated improvements if you like. You will probably decide that spending a lot of money is not necessary to have fun with **EASY HOME WINEMAKING!**

ENJOY!

GLOSSARY

AIRLOCK—a one-way device which allows gas to escape during fermentation, but which will not allow the entrance of impurities

AGING—the passage of time while wine remains in the barrel

AROMATIZE—the addition of herbs and spices to wine

BOUQUET—the fragrance of a mature wine

CARBON DIOXIDE—the gas formed during the fermentation process

CHARACTER—a combination of bouquet, clarity, crispness, color, and taste that distinguishes one wine from another

CO_2—carbon dioxide, the gas formed during fermentation

CONNOISSEUR—one who is, or professes to be, an expert on wines

DRY—wine that contains little or no sugar

FERMENTATION—the conversion of sugar into alcohol and carbon dioxide by the action of yeast

FORTIFIED—a wine that has increased alcoholic content due to the addition, after fermentation, of distilled spirits

HEAVY—a wine with an alcoholic content greater than fourteen percent. Also used to describe the body of a wine

LIGHT—a wine with an alcoholic content of less than fourteen percent. Also used to describe the body of a wine

MASH—a fermentable mixture that can be distilled into alcohol or spirits

MUST—the juice of the grape after it has begun fermentation

POLISH—the clarity and transparency of a fine wine

SPARKLING—wine which contains carbon dioxide gas

SWEET—wine that has unconverted sugar remaining, or that has had sugar added after fermentation

STILL—wine that contains no carbon dioxide gas

VINEGAR—wine that has been spoiled by undesirable yeasts, or wine that has aged too long

VINEYARD—ground planted with cultivated grapevines

VINTAGE—the yield of wine from a particular vineyard during a particular year

WINERY—an establishment where wine is produced

YEAST—any of various fungi capable of fermenting carbohydrates

INDEX

Wine

NOTES/RECIPES

ALL AMERICAN LIBRARY

Available, or soon-to-be released publications of ALL AMERICAN PRESS, P.O. Box 20773, Birmingham, AL 35216

BUSINESS & ENTREPRENEURSHIP

EFFECTIVE LETTER WRITING
EXECUTIVE'S PC SURVIVAL COURSE
SELF PUBLISHING MADE EASY
SELL YOUR BOOK BY MAIL

COOKBOOKS

ALL AMERICAN COOKBOOK

CONSUMER AFFAIRS

HOW TO GET YOUR MONEY'S WORTH

FUN

EASY HOME WINEMAKING
HOW TO MAKE HOMEBREW

HEALTH & FITNESS

OVERWEIGHT? IT'S ALL IN YOUR MIND
BEGINNING JOGGER'S HANDBOOK

PHOTOGRAPHY

HOW TO TAKE **ASTONISHING!** PET
   PORTRAITS
MACROPHOTOGRAPHY MADE EASY
HOW TO BUILD A HOME DARKROOM